YOUR KNOWLEDGE HAS VALUE

AF131299

- We will publish your bachelor's and master's thesis, essays and papers

- Your own eBook and book - sold worldwide in all relevant shops

- Earn money with each sale

Upload your text at www.GRIN.com and publish for free

Camille Boelen

Critical Book Review of "Humanity working" by David Erdal

Employee ownership and implications for the future of Human Resource Management

GRIN Verlag

Bibliografische Information der Deutschen Nationalbibliothek:

Die Deutsche Bibliothek verzeichnet diese Publikation in der Deutschen National-
bibliografie; detaillierte bibliografische Daten sind im Internet über http://dnb.d-
nb.de/ abrufbar.

Imprint:

Copyright © 2013 GRIN Verlag GmbH
Druck und Bindung: Books on Demand GmbH, Norderstedt Germany
ISBN: 978-3-656-82228-8

This book at GRIN:

http://www.grin.com/en/e-book/282387/critical-book-review-of-humanity-working-
by-david-erdal

GRIN - Your knowledge has value

Der GRIN Verlag publiziert seit 1998 wissenschaftliche Arbeiten von Studenten, Hochschullehrern und anderen Akademikern als eBook und gedrucktes Buch. Die Verlagswebsite www.grin.com ist die ideale Plattform zur Veröffentlichung von Hausarbeiten, Abschlussarbeiten, wissenschaftlichen Aufsätzen, Dissertationen und Fachbüchern.

Visit us on the internet:

http://www.grin.com/

http://www.facebook.com/grincom

http://www.twitter.com/grin_com

SCHOOL OF MANAGEMENT

Taught Postgraduate Programmes

Critical Book Review

Title of the book: Beyond the corporation: Humanity working

Author: David Erdal

Date of Publication: 2011

Publisher: The Bodley Head, Random House, London

Pages: 1-252.

« The more equal and involved community gave people longer, happier lives » (Erdal, 2011: 242). 'Beyond the corporation: Humanity working' is a factual and policy text of our modern economic system, in which David Erdal proposes to extend democracy into organisations, contributing to a better distribution of wealth. As a consequence, this view raises substantial economic, political and social debates. It is essential to indicate that the book was published not long after the financial crisis of 2008, which provides the author with an ideal context for supporting organic growth rather than seeking investment through capital markets. David Erdal has progressively built his credentials in the area of humanity working and Human egalitarianism. Starting from leveraging an employee buyout of his family business and being awarded the Scottish Business Achievement Award in 1989, he has then undertaken considerable procedures in creating an Employee Stock Ownership Plan (ESOP). Principally, David Erdal challenges the traditional economists' approaches to organisational ownership structures, aiming at denouncing the immorality of current practices. Contrastingly, he promotes, in an easy and strong language, the benefits of employee ownership structures to society as a whole and the reason why this practice should be developed, which forms the purpose of this book. To support the feasibility of his thesis, Erdal draws upon personal experiences, through his family business, current business examples, such as John Lewis, but also through substantial academic references.

Throughout this review, we will firstly explore the key questions that Erdal raises and their implications into contemporary and policy debates. Secondly, we will perform an integrative analysis of the book structure and assumptions made, and thirdly we will provide a critical assessment of the author's conclusions.

In today's highly precarious political and economic context, Erdal serves the interests of society as a whole, where highly committed employees will be able to complete themselves in their professional lives. He does so, by defending the expansion of democracy in the business world. Indeed, western societies have naturally organized themselves into the form of democracies; it is therefore natural that business follows the same evolution (Dahl, 1985:135 in Dow, 2003). It is even more natural to undertake this change as along with globalisation, operations in western economies have shifted from the need of factories to human intellect and collaboration (Blasi et al., 2003). Indeed, McKinsey's managing director endorses the fact that a new economic system is primordial for our economy to prosper (Caulkin, 2011). As Kramer states in Caulkin's article, 'shared value' is fundamental for our economic development. Derrick and Phipps claim that it is a « natural moral law » and indeed, it is tough to recognise that 'capitalism' today, is perceived as 'normal'. Hence, the major question is who should benefit from employees' sweat?

By suggesting this new economic system, Erdal is convinced that it will result in a proportionate distribution of wealth. Hence, the author challenges traditional top-down organisations that seek investment through capital markets and thus, maximize speculation and the risk of financial crisis. Indeed, investors don't really 'care' about the business itself but are exclusively interested in capital gain (Derrick & Phipps, 1969). Undeniably, Erdal argues that seeking organic growth through employee ownership structures is the only way to prosperity. He argues that the productivity achieved by workers would no longer enrich capital markets but will be reinvested in the business itself. This view greatly differs from the economists' perspectives for which investors play a key role in the development of our economy. Subsequently, managers are focusing on shareholders at the expense of labour and consumers. In contrast, seeing labour as an asset rather than a cost would enable organisations to gain core competencies (Torrington et al. 2011) and thus, achieve sustainable competitive advantage (Porter & Kramer, 2011). Yet, in order to gain core competencies, it is essential to implement core job characteristics represented in Figure 1. In doing so, it may provide workers with a true sense of responsibility and thus, contributing to greater commitment and leading to better outcomes.

Figure 1 : The Job Characteristics Model

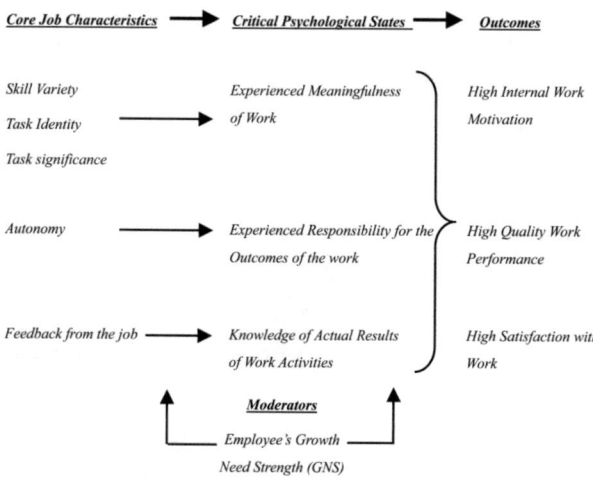

Adapted from Hackman and Oldham (1980)

These core job characteristics expresses the 'workforce philosophy' of which one can witness to what degree employees are valued in a company (Kaarsemaker & Poutsma, 2006), which is specifically the approach that Erdal is aiming to establish.

However, there are some key concerns about employee owned companies. Firstly, not all employees are eligible (Pérotin & Robinson, 2002), some might refuse to take responsibilities or prefer to be passive. Secondly, Erdal talks about 'employee owned' companies but Dow (2003) argues that it is not correct to claim that firms can be owned as a firm is a 'set of human agents' and therefore, not an instrument as such. Accordingly, Dow uses the word 'Labour Managed Firm'.

In terms of structure, Erdal takes a progressive view in four distinctive steps before establishing his conclusions.

First, investigating and relating real life examples of employee-owned companies, contrasting these with assumptions made by traditional economists. Indeed, Erdal argues that their assumptions are rather more theoretical than practical as these are based on predictions and theory and therefore, uses real life examples that specifically undermine these predictions.

4

The second part of the book, help shed light on the reality of traditional employment and especially the reality of human selfishness and restricted view on desired outcomes. Indeed, a lot of procedures and laws have been developed according to the debates that arose from the unconditional 'war' of owners and workers. Nowadays, political parties as well as economists are still debating upon these laws and are constantly trying to find new ways of operating. Consequently, a way of ending this infinite war, may be for politicians and legal profession, to develop and encourage employee-owned companies so that employee themselves can feel the implications and responsibilities of being an owner. There is therefore a need for a general « social maturity » for the system to work (Derrick & Phipps, 1969). This way, unions would stop fighting for conditions of work, wages and other matters (Derrick & Phipps, 1969). The reality is that today, capitalism is stuck between maintaining shareholder value as well as satisfying constant employment laws, arising from the trade unions revolts, that are weighing on organisational productivity. Therefore, it is a question of seeing the bigger picture as well as showing integrity and fairness.

The third part of the book intends to give guidelines onto how to implement successful employee owned companies; bringing in benefits, functions and challenges of employee owned structures, hereby demonstrating their contributions to high performance. However, there seems to be a lack of empirical evidence on the relationship between employee owned structures and human resource activities (Kaarsemaker & Poutsma, 2006). Nonetheless, the implementation of five core HR practices listed in Table 1 seem to provide workers with a true sense of ownership and thus, contributes to high performance:

TABLE 1
Translation of Ownership Rights into Organizational Practices

Ownership Rights	Corporate Governance Practices	HRM Practices
Use	• Voting rights • Shareholders' meetings • Board membership	• Participation in decision-making • Information sharing • Training for business literacy • Mediation
Returns	• Dividends • Share price	• Profit sharing
Sale	• Simply decide to sell shares	• Participation in decision-making about employee ownership • Sharing of information with regard to employee ownership • Training for business literacy to understand and be capable of the above

Kaarsemaker & Poutsma, 2006

As Blasi et al. claim, less than 2% of companies choose as a HR practice, the involvement of the majority of their employees in decision-making. Presumably, it is rational to think that if companies embraces these five HR practices and involve their employees in the design of systems and structures, the company will naturally reflect a common identity, and thus, create a resilient system.

Finally, the Fourth part concludes on the constitution of human nature and how employee ownership can serve society for the greater good. Although no studies have shown that this concept can be applied universally, it is a natural organisation of society which is therefore likely to function in most cultures. However, although this economic system may not even be convenient in certain industries (Dow, 2003), Erdal is maintaining a purpose of morality.

In inquiring into the meaning of this book, it is hard not to agree with the author. The actual facts that he denounces are all around us and are perceived to be normal when it is just a narrow-minded view of economic systems. It may be that people unconsciously benefit society by seeking their personal well-being as Adam Smiths' 'invisible hand' suggests (The Economist, 2013), but structuring systems according to the greater benefit, could lead to prosperity in an equal society. There is a need for political parties to encourage employee buyouts when the CEO retires or in the case of judicial liquidation and help create financial institutions aimed at funding employee-owned companies.

Furthermore, as McKinsey's global managing director claims in Caulkin's article, the ignorance of the social aspects in current management practices has highly contributed to the financial crisis. Therefore, there is also a need for consultants and business schools to contribute in shaping the design of an increasingly balanced economic system. Indeed, Management schools can contribute in developing future business coaches who have the capacity to develop workers as leaders themselves. The John Lewis example may well inspire HR professionals to work in such a structure, where managers are perceived as coaches. This means that they are rather more spending their time developing people interactions and improving HR practices according to encompassing dynamics, than repairing effects of contentious relationships. This is often the result of perceiving labour as a cost rather than an asset (Legge, 2005).

Essentially, it is rational to assume that commitment of the whole leads to better outcomes as it may foster innovation through the diversity of ideas that are stemmed from the leadership of everyone at hand. Indeed, everyone has the potential to become a leader in what they are passionate about and it is a shame if this continues to be killed by capitalist authorities. In fact, the more people care about what they do, the more they feel responsible for what they achieve. Following this logic, the scandal about horse meat for instance, wouldn't have occurred. Many other global issues, such as the Concordia or the collapse of the factory in Bangladesh, would be prevented by taking an approach that promotes dignity and respect.

However, it seems that David Erdal doesn't anticipate the effects of this approach. Indeed, this approach should promote internal growth and thereby, increase health and consumption. How could we then design a resilient aging system? How can we handle at the same time our lack of resources? If we are to implement democracy in the workplace, we should, naturally, seek complementarities and synergies in order to implement a 'creative institutional design' (Dow, 2003), but we should, more importantly, anticipate the effects of this approach.

To conclude, the key questions that David Erdal raises in his thesis, provides an interesting alternative to our current economic system. The structure of the book enables to progressively understand by what means the author comes to such conclusions and leaves us with no other alternative than consentient. Indeed, it is obvious that a new economic system is fundamental for our prosperity and employee ownership structures may well be the natural way forward. This way, the wealth created by organisations will be reinvested in the business, which should enable a natural and progressive evolution.

Additionally, it is undeniable that traditional economists' theories are aiming at enriching capital markets as opposed to promoting a proportionate distribution of wealth. Indeed, seeking ways of making money by impoverishing others doesn't provide us with happiness; in fact, it is about caring for the greater good of humanity so as to achieve prosperity on the whole. Undoubtedly, workers should have the right to participate in the decision-making and the design of systems and practices, not only for a purpose of rationality, such as motivation and commitment, but more importantly for a question of morality. This is the reason why political parties, the legal profession, consultants and business schools should support and contribute in implementing this change. However, the author doesn't provide us with an anticipation plan and thus, leads us to question the consequences and implications of this approach. Nonetheless, the combination of humanity and morality aspects in David Erdal's book are strongly inspiring and should be appreciated by many.

Bibliography

Blasi, J., Kruse, D., Bernstein, A. (2003). *In the Company of Owners : The Truth about Stock Options (and Why Every Employee Should Have Them)*. Basic Books, A Member of the Perseus Books Group.

Caulkin, S. (2011) Saving Capitalism from itself. *Management Today.*

Colbert, B.A. (2004) 'The Complex Resource-Based View: Implications for Theory and Practice in Strategic Human Resource Management', *Academy of Management Review* 29(3): 341-58

Dahl, R. A. (1985) A preface to Economic Democracy, *University of California Press*, Berkeley.

Derrick, P., Phipps, J.-F. (1969) *Co-ownership Co-operation and control : an industrial objective.* Longmans, Green and Co Ltd : London

Dow, G.K. (2003). *Governing the Firm : Workers' Control in Theory and Practice.* The press syndicate of the University of Cambridge. Cambridge.

Ecb.europa.eu. 2013. BCE: Timelime of the financial crisis. [online] Available at: http://www.ecb.europa.eu/ecb/html/crisis.fr.html [Accessed: 2 Oct 2013].

Erdal, D. (2011) *Beyond the Corporation: Humanity Working.* London: The Bodley Head, Random House. 1-252.

Garg, P., Rastogi, R. (2006) "New model of job design: motivating employees' performance", *Emerald 25.*

Hackman, J.R. and Oldham, G.R. (1980) *Work Redesign.* New York: Addison-Wesley.

Kaarsemaker, E.C.A., Poutsma, E. (2006) The Fit of Employee Ownership with Other Human Resource Management Practices : Theoretical and Empirical Suggestions Regarding the Existence of an Ownership High-Performance Work System. *Economic and Industrial Democracy*, Vol. 27(4) : 669-685.

Kinnie, N. & Swart, J. Human Resource Management and Organisational Performance (Chapter 2) In: Redman, T. & Wilkinson, A. (2009) Contemporary Human Resource Management: Text and Cases (3rd ed), London, FT-Prentice Hall.

Legge, K. (2005) Human Resource Management, Rhetorics and Realities. Palgrave Macmillan, New York.

Pérotin, V., Robinson, A. (2002) Employee Participation in Profit and Ownership: A Review of the issues and Evidence. Leeds University Business School. 1- 28.

Porter, M., Kramer, M. (2011) How to Fix Capitalism and unleash a new wave of growth. *Harvard Business Review.* 1-17.

Schuler, R.S. (1992) 'Strategic Human Resources Management: Linking the People with the Strategic Needs of the Business', Organizational Dynamics 21(1): 18-32.

The Economist (2013). A little help from the invisible hand. [online] Available at: http://www.economist.com/node/21564594 [Accessed: 2 Oct 2013].

Torrington, D., Hall, L., Taylor, S. and Atkinson, C. (2011) Human Resource Management (8th ed). London, FT Prentice Hall.